One
Pound
Meals

PHOTOGRAPHY
DAN JONES

DESIGN
SUPERFANTASTIC

MIGUEL BARCLAY'S

ONE POUND MEALS

SUPER EASY

www.onepoundmeals.com

CONTENTS

As most of you know, there are no chapters in my books. I'd rather you flicked through and picked what you like the look of. But, if you have something specific in mind, here is a list of all the recipes in the book.

#VEGETARIAN

#FISHANDSEAFOOD

Black Rice **156**

Couscous Paella **32**

Curried Fish
& Leek Noodles **148**

Fisherman's Macaroni Pie **18**

Mega Spring Roll **130**

Oven Dim Sum **112**

Poke Bowl **144**

Prawn & Lentil Curry **114**

Prawn Thermidor **180**

Smoked Mackerel
& Kale Carbonara **102**

White Fish Chowder **150**

#MEAT

Asian Stuffed Peppers **60**

Bacon & White Bean
No-Blend Soup **118**

BBQ Lentils & Bacon **84**

Beef Stroganoff Pasta **46**

Cabbage Wraps **44**

Cheese & Potato Hotpot **196**

Cheesy Ham & Leek Pie **98**

Chilli Lamb Noodles **82**

Chinese Bok Choi **176**

Chorizo BBQ Beans **16**

Chorizo Dumplings **110**

Cubetti Hotpot **168**

Detroit Pizza **194**

Filo Nachos **62**

Ham & Leek Risotto **42**

Keema Lamb Tacos **92**

Lamb Kofte Burger **22**

Leek, Peas, Bacon
& Cream **28**

One-Pan Lasagne **76**

One-Pan Sausage
& Apple **54**

Ragu Di Porco **200**

Roast Pork Belly **142**

Sausage & Black Bean
Stir-Fry **30**

Sausage & Polenta Bake **40**

Sausage Cassoulet **58**

Savoury Lamb Baklava **192**

Sloppy Giuseppe **132**

Slow-Roast Rendang **48**

Sprout Caesar Salad **164**

Stilton Sausage Rolls **34**

#CHICKEN

5-Clove Chicken **116**

Arroz De Campo **122**

Chicken & Creamed
Spinach **152**

Chicken & Potato in a
Creamy Sauce **166**

Chicken Iskender **86**

Chicken Parmigiana **188**

Glazed Chicken
& Sweet Pea Stir-Fry **72**

Peri Peri Tacos **202**

Turmeric Chicken Biryani **52**

SO, WHAT'S NEXT FOR ONE POUND MEALS?

Firstly, thank you so much for buying my book. I can't believe that it has only been two years since I posted my very first One Pound Meal on Instagram. I hope that I've helped inspire you guys to get cooking and that you've enjoyed the journey with me so far.

I've had an amazing few months writing this book and it might actually be my favourite one yet! I took everything I learnt from creating my first two books and really focused on what One Pound Meals has come to mean to people. Since the launch of my first book, a book that proved you could cook delicious meals for under £1, One Pound Meals has evolved far beyond making meals for a pound – it has become a way of cooking. Simple ingredients, straightforward recipes, mouthwatering dishes – this is now an everyday style of cooking that is helping to inspire thousands of people to start cooking quicker and healthier meals from scratch at home.

MY NEW CHALLENGE

Whenever I speak to people about cooking from scratch at home, the number-one excuse I always hear is 'I don't want all that washing up'. And I totally get it. If you're only cooking one portion of food and it takes longer to wash up than it takes to eat it, then I'd also be tempted to order a takeaway or buy a ready-meal. So the challenge for me, in my mission to get more people cooking from scratch at home, was to eliminate as much washing up as possible. I set about creating the ultimate set of £1 recipes that used only one pan, one pot or one tray, and hopefully writing the most useful cookbook you'll ever own; a book that will inspire you to say 'I'll make that tonight' because you know it'll be quick, thrifty, delicious and super easy.

So, my new recipes in this book have even more shortcuts than ever, more clever hacks and cheats, but most importantly, way less washing up, so there really is no excuse now.

A WARNING
TO RECIPE SNOBS

I have to be honest and confess that I've taken all those traditional long-winded recipes that chefs and home cooks have been faithfully following for centuries and well and truly thrown them out of the window. I'm dreading what my Spanish grandma will say when she sees my 10-minute paella made with couscous, or when someone from Napoli sees my puff pastry pizza. But the fact is, who wants to spend three hours in the kitchen after a hard day's work? This is cooking for people who live in the 21st century. Realistic recipes for people who still want to cook from scratch using fresh ingredients, but just don't have much time.

SIMPLER RECIPES

I started my journey by first taking all my favourite classics like lasagne, paella and pizza, then reworking them and taking huge shortcuts. So, I immediately reduced the lasagne to one layer, substituted the rice in my paella for couscous and made a few different pizzas using puff pastry, then self-raising flour and then even using no pizza base at all. I had so much fun inventing different shortcuts, then I got to work creating whole new recipes using exactly the same principles. The key was to find a way to cook the carbs alongside the veg, the meat and the sauce. So, dishes like my £1 biryani, where the rice, peas and chicken cook together in one pot were perfect. I then started adding potatoes and lentils to curries so that I didn't need to cook a separate pot of rice and this then evolved into boiling eggs in the same pan that I was cooking the noodles in. I was going shortcut crazy!

THE SAME PHILOSOPHY

Even though this book is an evolution of my first *One Pound Meals* book, I still wanted to keep to the same original principles, so firstly, and most importantly, every recipe was kept to a £1 budget. I also wanted to stick to the same core group of ingredients to make it easier to eliminate waste through overlapping of ingredients across all three books. Also, by cooking from scratch, we are able to control our salt, sugar and preservatives intake, and this is an important aspect of One Pound Meals because cooking from scratch is a way more healthy alternative to eating convenience and takeaway foods. All I've really changed for this book is to double up on the shortcuts and make much easier recipes with minimal washing up.

As with my first two books, *Super Easy* still uses exactly the same set of common supermarket ingredients and this is key to eating on a budget. The idea behind this is firstly that these ingredients are the 'loss leaders' or items that are sold with very little premium added. All supermarkets are competing for who has the cheapest Cheddar cheese or the cheapest cauliflowers, so I take advantage of this and create my recipes around these products. And secondly, you need to be armed with multiple recipes for every single ingredient you're intending to buy if you are to have any chance of eliminating waste. Realistically, you'll never eat a whole block of feta in one go, and if you throw half of it away, then you've technically paid double for it. So, across all three of my books, there must be well over 20 recipes that use feta cheese, helping to keep your meals varied, exciting, and most importantly, waste-free.

I hope you find this book useful, and please don't forget to tag me in your Instagram posts because it always makes me so happy to see you cooking my recipes at home.

Enjoy,

Miguel

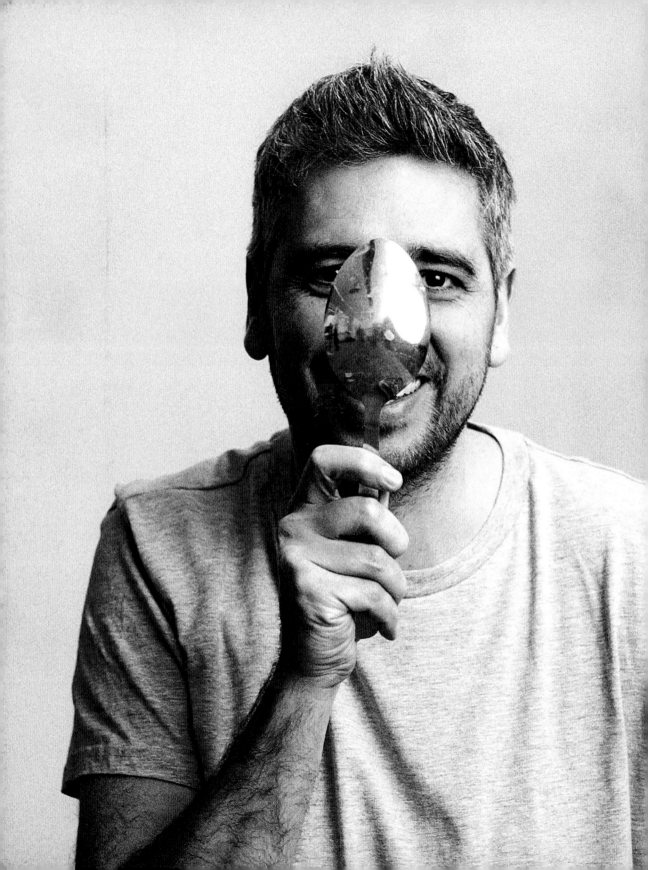

ALL RECIPES
ARE FOR A SINGLE
SERVING

Remember that all my recipes are for one person.

MORE THAN ONE PERSON?

Just multiply the ingredients – because they are so
straightforward, it's no trouble at all to calculate.

CHORIZO BBQ BEANS

This is one of my favourite brunches ever: smoky BBQ beans with chorizo on sourdough. It's as hearty as a fry-up but takes a fraction of the time and effort. After eating this, you'll realise that normal baked beans just no longer fit the bill.

To make 1 portion

A few slices of cooking chorizo

¼ red onion, sliced

100g cannellini beans (from a 400g tin), drained

50g passata (from a 400g tin)

Pinch of ground cumin

Pinch of smoked paprika

1 tbsp tomato ketchup

Slice of sourdough bread

Olive oil

Salt and pepper

To cook

Pan-fry the chorizo in a splash of olive oil over a medium heat for a couple of minutes then add the onion and fry for a further couple of minutes until soft. Add the beans, passata, cumin, paprika and ketchup, season with salt and pepper and simmer for about 5 minutes until the sauce is thick and sticky.

Meanwhile, lightly toast the bread.

Pour the BBQ beans and chorizo over the bread and sprinkle with some cracked black pepper.

FISHERMAN'S MACARONI PIE

This is a wholesome hunger-busting dish that uses a few of my favourite shortcuts to ensure it can be cooked in just one pan. By using a breadcrumb topping instead of mashed potato, adding uncooked macaroni, frozen fish and frozen peas, I've created a simple and easy recipe that you'll cook over and over again.

To make I portion

1 tbsp butter

1 tsp plain flour

300ml milk

Handful of macaroni

1 frozen white fish fillet

Handful of frozen peas

Stale bread, torn into small chunks

Olive oil

Salt and pepper

To cook

Grab an ovenproof pan*, add the butter and melt it over a medium heat. Stir in the flour to create a paste and cook for a further minute. Gradually add the milk, stirring continuously, and cook until you have a smooth sauce. Throw in the macaroni and simmer for a few minutes then add the frozen fish. Cook for about 10 minutes until the fish has defrosted and is cooked and flaky, season with salt and pepper, add the frozen peas and continue to cook for 2 more minutes.

Remove from the heat and sprinkle the bread chunks over the filling, along with a pinch of salt, some cracked black pepper and a generous glug of olive oil.

Finish the pie under a hot grill for a few minutes until the breadcrumbs are nice and golden brown.

* If you don't have a pan with an ovenproof handle, then just use your normal pan and transfer the filling to an ovenproof dish before adding the breadcrumb top.

THAI OMELETTE

The key to making this dish special is to add a small pinch of curry powder to the beaten egg. This immediately transforms a regular omelette into a fancy Thai-style street food delicacy.

To make 1 portion

3 eggs, beaten

Pinch of curry powder

Sesame oil

¼ carrot, cut into matchsticks

½ spring onion, cut into strips

A few beansprouts

Drizzle of soy sauce

Salt and pepper

To cook

Season the beaten eggs with salt, pepper and the curry powder.

Heat a splash of sesame oil in a frying pan, pour in the beaten eggs and fry for a few minutes until 80% cooked, then add the carrot, spring onion and beansprouts to the middle, drizzle over a little sesame oil and soy sauce, then fold the omelette over the filling and continue to cook for another minute. Remove from the heat and serve with another drizzle of soy sauce to finish.

LAMB KOFTE BURGER

One day I was thinking about how amazing it would be to have a burger that was actually a lamb kofte, and a bun that was actually a pitta. I started testing out a few recipe ideas, and as soon as I crumbled some feta cheese on one of the burgers, I knew it had to go into my book.

To make 1 portion

100g minced lamb

1 garlic clove, crushed

1 tsp ground cumin

½ red onion, ¼ of it very finely diced, the rest sliced

80g self-raising flour, plus extra for dusting

50ml cold water

Lettuce

1 slice of tomato

Small amount of feta cheese, crumbled

Olive oil

Salt and pepper

To cook

Mix together the lamb, garlic and cumin with the finely diced red onion and season with salt and pepper. Form the mixture into a patty. Grease the patty on both sides with olive oil. Heat a dry griddle pan or frying pan over a medium-high heat and, when hot, add the patty and fry for about 6 minutes on each side until cooked through.

While the lamb patty is cooking, make the pitta dough. Mix the self-raising flour and water in a bowl with a big pinch of salt to form a dough. Knead on a floured work surface for a couple of minutes until you get a smooth dough, then cut it in half and shape each piece into a bun-sized circle. Wipe the griddle pan or frying pan with kitchen paper, add the pittas and cook for a couple of minutes on each side until risen, toasted and cooked through.

Assemble the kofte burger by stacking the lettuce, tomato, sliced onion, the lamb patty and crumbled feta cheese on one of the pittas and topping with the second toasted pitta.

CHEESE & TOMATO PUFF PASTRY QUICHE

Imagine how many more quiches you'd make if it wasn't such a time-consuming process. Well, now there's no excuse. Here, the pastry is pre-made and you don't need to sweat down any onions: just throw the raw ingredients together and bake.

To make 1 portion

1 square of puff pastry

3 eggs, beaten

Handful of grated Cheddar cheese

A few cherry tomatoes, halved

Olive oil

Salt and pepper

To cook

Preheat your oven to 190°C/gas mark 5.

Grease an ovenproof dish or pan with oil, cut the puff pastry to roughly fit (don't worry about trimming the edges), then line the dish or pan with it.

Combine the beaten eggs and grated cheese and season with salt and pepper. Pour the mixture into the dish or pan, then top with the tomato halves, cut-side up. To get a lovely golden crust, brush some of the egg filling onto the edges of the pastry, then bake in the oven for about 30 minutes until the pastry is golden brown and the filling is set.

Remove the quiche from the oven, sprinkle with salt and pepper, and serve hot or cold.

BEETROOT CURRY

Ever wondered what else you can make with beetroot? This is my super-easy Beetroot Curry, made lighter and healthier by using crème fraîche. Ready in minutes, it's packed with all the flavour and goodness of beetroot.

To make 1 portion

½ red onion, cut into wedges

1 pre-cooked beetroot, cut into wedges

1 tsp curry powder

2 tbsp crème fraîche

Pinch of dried chilli flakes

Olive oil

Salt and pepper

To cook

Pan-fry the onion and beetroot in a splash of olive oil over a medium heat. After about 5 minutes, once the onion has softened, stir in the curry powder and make sure everything is evenly coated. Cook for 1 minute, then add the crème fraîche, salt and pepper and simmer for a couple more minutes.

Serve in a bowl garnished with the chilli flakes.

LEEK, PEAS, BACON & CREAM

Eat this lovely fresh and vibrant dish straight out of the pan on a relaxing summer's afternoon with a glass of white wine.

To make 1 portion

½ leek, cut into circles

1 tsp butter

3 rashers of smoked streaky bacon, cut into thirds

Handful of frozen peas

150ml single cream

Olive oil

Salt and pepper

To cook

Pan-fry the leek in a splash of olive oil with the butter over a medium heat, turning occasionally so it cooks evenly. After about 5 minutes, as the leeks start to brown, throw in the bacon and fry for a further 4 minutes until the bacon is cooked. Next, add the peas, season with salt and pepper and continue to pan-fry for a further minute until the peas have defrosted. Add the cream and simmer for a minute or two to thicken the sauce slightly. Season again, to taste, and serve with a drizzle of olive oil.

SAUSAGE & BLACK BEAN STIR-FRY

You wouldn't usually think about using sausage in a stir-fry but, when you complement it with black beans, garlic and soy sauce, you get an exceptional depth of flavour that makes this dish a taste explosion.

To make 1 portion

2 sausages

Sesame oil

1 garlic clove, sliced

A few dried chillies (or dried chilli flakes)

200g black beans (from a 400g tin), drained

Splash of soy sauce

Handful of green beans

Salt and pepper

To cook

Cut the sausage skins, squeeze out the meat and pan-fry it in a splash of sesame oil over a medium heat, breaking it up into chunks with a wooden spoon, for about 5 minutes. When the sausagemeat starts to brown, throw in the garlic and continue to fry for a few minutes. When the garlic starts to brown, add the dried chillies, black beans, soy sauce, green beans and a splash of water. Simmer for about 4 minutes until the beans are soft and the sauce has reduced slightly. Remove from the heat, season with salt and pepper, a splash more soy sauce if required, and a tiny drizzle of sesame oil, then serve.

COUSCOUS PAELLA

This dish has classic paella flavours but takes only 10 minutes to make. That's some seriously fast cooking! Using couscous instead of rice eliminates most of the hassle involved in making a real paella and simplifies the whole dish to a couple of easy steps.

To make 1 portion

¼ red pepper, cut into strips

Small handful of cooked and peeled prawns

Small handful of frozen peas

Pinch of turmeric

½ chicken stock cube

1 egg-cup of couscous

Olive oil

Salt and pepper

To cook

Pan-fry the pepper in a splash of olive oil over a medium heat. After a couple of minutes add the prawns, peas and turmeric, crumble in the stock cube and add a small splash of water (about 1 egg-cup). Simmer for a couple of minutes until the peas are cooked and half the water has evaporated.

Remove from the heat, season with salt and pepper and stir in the couscous. Leave for a minute and it will plump up to create this amazing Couscous Paella.

STILTON SAUSAGE ROLLS

Inside these sausage rolls is a hidden stilton cheese centre, which gives these homemade treats an extra kick and an amazing depth of flavour.

To make 4

2 sausages

4 cubes of stilton, about the size of a dice

4 rectangles of puff pastry, about 8 x 4cm each

Milk, for brushing

Pinch of sesame seeds

1 tsp English mustard

To cook

Preheat your oven to 190°C/gas mark 5 and line a baking tray with greaseproof paper.

Cut the sausage skins, squeeze out the meat and divide it into 4 equal portions. Wrap each piece of stilton with sausagemeat, then wrap each sausagemeat portion in a piece of puff pastry, using the back of a fork to press the pastry edges together to seal (you can leave the filling exposed on the sides). Place them on the lined baking tray.

Brush the sausage rolls with milk, sprinkle with the sesame seeds and bake in the oven for 30 minutes or until the pastry is golden brown and the sausagemeat is cooked through.

Remove from the oven and serve with a dollop of mustard.

#vegetarian #curry

SWEET & HOT AUBERGINE

Here's a gorgeously sticky, sweet and hot curry that will blow you away. It's an easy one-pan recipe that balances wildly contrasting flavours using simple storecupboard ingredients.

To make 1 portion

¼ aubergine, cut into chunks

Sesame oil

½ red onion, cut into circles

1 garlic clove, sliced

A few dried chillies (or dried chilli flakes)

Squeeze of honey

Soy sauce

1 tbsp chicken (or veg) gravy granules

Splash of water

½ spring onion, thinly sliced

Salt and pepper

To cook

Pan-fry the aubergine in a splash of sesame oil over a medium heat for 8 minutes, then add the onion, garlic, dried chillies, a splash more sesame oil, season with salt and pepper and fry for a few more minutes. Add the honey, a splash of soy sauce, gravy granules and water to create a sticky sauce and cook for a minute or two to make the sauce even stickier. Garnish with the sliced spring onion and serve.

BANG BANG CAULIFLOWER

My £1 Bang Bang Cauliflower has all the familiar Chinese-style sweet and spicy flavours but is a delicious and healthy alternative to those expensive takeaways.

To make 1 portion

Handful of cauliflower florets

1 garlic clove, sliced

Pinch of dried chilli flakes

Sesame oil

100g passata (from a 400g tin)

2 tbsp honey

Pinch of sesame seeds

½ spring onion, sliced

Salt and pepper

To cook

Grab a saucepan, throw in the cauliflower florets, garlic and chilli flakes, season with salt and pepper, then fry in a splash of sesame oil over a medium heat. Just before the garlic starts to brown, add the passata and honey. Simmer for 5–10 minutes until the liquid reduces and sticks to the cauliflower, adding a tiny splash of water if the sauce gets too thick. Once the cauliflower is soft, remove the pan from the heat and serve it with a sprinkle of sesame seeds, a drizzle of sesame oil and a garnish of sliced spring onion.

SAUSAGE & POLENTA BAKE

I knew there had to be a simple way of cooking polenta, so I devised this huge shortcut to create a tasty oven-baked polenta dish that requires just 2 minutes prep and no stirring or checking while it's cooking.

To make 1 portion

1 egg-cup of polenta

4 egg-cups of milk

1 sausage

A few cherry tomatoes (on the vine)

Olive oil

Salt and pepper

To cook

Preheat your oven to 190°C/gas mark 5.

Put the polenta and milk in an ovenproof dish or pan. Season with salt and pepper, stir, then throw in the sausage and the tomatoes.

Bake in the oven for about 35 minutes until the sausage is nicely browned, then serve garnished with cracked black pepper and a glug of olive oil.

HAM & LEEK RISOTTO

It's annoying when you have to keep two pans on the go just to make a risotto: one for the rice and another to keep the stock bubbling away. So here I have created a recipe that requires just one pan and a kettle.

To make 1 portion

½ leek, sliced

Handful of arborio rice

½ chicken stock cube

Kettle of boiling water

Slice of thick-cut ham, torn into chunks

Handful of grated parmesan

Olive oil

Salt and pepper

To cook

Pan-fry the leek in a splash of olive oil over a medium heat. Once softened, stir in the arborio rice and season with salt and pepper. Next, crumble in the stock cube and add 100ml of the boiling water, then stir continuously as the rice starts to plump up. Gradually add more water little by little (you'll use about 400ml in total), continuing to stir, and after about 15 minutes the rice should be cooked but still firm. Remove from the heat and stir in the ham and grated parmesan. Season once more if required, drizzle over a little olive oil and serve.

CABBAGE WRAPS

These cabbage wraps are so easy to make, and they look stunning against the vibrant red tomato sauce. With the sausagemeat and mushroom stuffing, all the flavours and seasoning are pretty much taken care of, making this even easier to get spot-on each time.

To make 1 portion

3 Savoy cabbage leaves

1 sausage

½ red onion, sliced

Small handful of mushrooms, finely diced

200g passata (from a 400g tin)

Olive oil

Salt and pepper

To cook

Preheat your oven to 190°C/gas mark 5.

Soften the cabbage leaves in a heatproof bowl of just-boiled water for 10 minutes while you prepare the filling.

Cut the sausage skin, squeeze out the meat and mix it in a bowl with the sliced onion and mushrooms. Divide the filling into three equal portions.

Drain the cabbage leaves then put a portion of filling into each one before wrapping the leaves around the filling.

Grab an ovenproof dish and pour in the passata, season with salt and pepper and place the stuffed cabbage leaves on top. Drizzle with olive oil and bake in the oven for 30 minutes, until the sausage filling is cooked through, then serve.

BEEF STROGANOFF PASTA

I absolutely love the flavours of a stroganoff, so I decided to adapt the recipe from my first book slightly and create a simple one-pot pasta version with minced beef.

To make 1 portion

¼ onion, sliced

A few button mushrooms, sliced

75g minced beef

1 garlic clove, sliced

1 tsp paprika

½ beef stock cube

300ml water

100g pasta

50ml single cream

Small handful of spinach

Olive oil

Salt and pepper

To cook

Fry the onion and mushrooms gently in a saucepan with a splash of olive oil over a medium heat. Once the onion has softened, add the minced beef, season with salt and pepper and fry for about 5 minutes until it starts to brown, then add the garlic and cook for a few more minutes. Add the paprika then crumble in the stock cube and pour in the water. Bring to the boil, add the pasta and simmer until the pasta is cooked and the sauce has reduced. When the pasta is cooked, remove from the heat and stir in the cream and spinach. Season to taste, and once the spinach has wilted, you are ready to serve.

SLOW-ROAST RENDANG

By slowly cooking inexpensive cuts of meat to create luxurious and intensely flavoured dishes, it's definitely possible to eat like a king on a budget. This dish might take a bit of time to make, but there is very little prep involved: just throw it in the casserole dish and wait.

To make 1 portion

½ onion, sliced

1 pork shoulder steak

2 tsp curry powder

200g chopped tomatoes (from a 400g tin)

½ beef stock cube

Handful of green beans

Olive oil

Salt and pepper

To cook

Grab a saucepan or a casserole dish with a lid. Fry the onion in a splash of olive oil over a medium heat until softened, season with salt and pepper and throw in the pork, curry powder and chopped tomatoes and crumble in the stock cube. Cover and simmer over a low heat for about 3 hours.

Flake the meat apart using a fork and simmer uncovered for a further 30 minutes until the sauce has reduced to a thicker consistency. In the last 5 minutes of cooking, stir in the green beans and, as soon as they are tender, serve.

FETA & SUN-DRIED TOMATO FLATBAKES

These wafer-thin tarts have the most amazing crunch and are packed with the intense flavours of sun-dried tomatoes and baked feta cheese. Cut the folded filo to the exact dimensions of your lunchbox to take your packed lunches to the next level.

To make 1 portion

1 sheet of filo pastry

Small handful of feta cheese, crumbled

A few sun-dried tomatoes

Olive oil

Black pepper

To cook

Preheat your oven to 190°C/gas mark 5.

Fold the filo sheet to make it 3 layers thick, place it on a baking tray, then brush with olive oil and fold in the edges to create an area for the filling. Sprinkle the feta onto the filo and top with sun-dried tomatoes. Bake in the oven for about 15 minutes until the filo is golden brown, then garnish with plenty of cracked black pepper.

TURMERIC CHICKEN BIRYANI

My simplified version of a classic biryani has taken out all the superfluous ingredients and non-essential steps to create the easiest path from a few ingredients to a delicious plate of food.

To make 1 portion

2 chicken drumsticks

½ mug of basmati rice

1 mug of water

1 tsp ground turmeric

2 tsp curry powder

½ chicken stock cube

Handful of frozen peas

Pinch of flaked almonds

Olive oil

Salt and pepper

To cook

Grab a saucepan or casserole dish with a lid. Season the chicken legs with salt and pepper and fry them in the saucepan or casserole dish in a splash of olive oil over a medium heat for 15 minutes. Throw in the rice and add the water, turmeric and curry powder, then crumble in the stock cube. Cover and simmer gently over a low heat for about 10 minutes, then add the peas and cook for a further 5 minutes or so until the rice and chicken are cooked and all the water has been absorbed. Sprinkle over the flaked almonds then serve.

ONE-PAN SAUSAGE & APPLE

I love the classic combination of sausage and apple, especially when I can get a bit of caramelisation on the apple pieces by pan-frying them. So this is a quick one-pan recipe that balances these sweet and savoury flavours perfectly.

To make 1 portion

2 sausages

½ apple, sliced

½ red onion, sliced

Handful of shredded savoy cabbage

about 100ml water

1 tbsp beef gravy granules

Olive oil

Salt and pepper

To cook

Pan-fry the sausages in a splash of olive oil over a medium heat for about 15 minutes. When the sausages are just about cooked, add the sliced apple and onion and continue cooking for about 5 minutes before adding the cabbage and seasoning with salt and pepper. Cook for a further 3 minutes, then add the water along with the gravy granules, stir and simmer for a few minutes before serving.

VEGGIE BLACK BEAN CHILLI

For this dish I had to choose between black beans or classic kidney beans, but there was only one winner in my eyes. Black beans are the best shortcut to achieving those dark and rich Mexican flavours that usually take hours of simmering to create.

To make 1 portion

½ red onion, sliced

2 garlic cloves, sliced

½ red pepper, sliced

200g black beans (from a 400g tin)

A few dried chillies (or dried chilli flakes)

2 tsp ground cumin

200g chopped tomatoes (from a 400g tin)

1 tbsp crème fraîche

Olive oil

Salt and pepper

To cook

Pan-fry the onion in a splash of olive oil over a medium heat. Once softened, season with salt and pepper, then add the garlic and red pepper and cook for a couple of minutes until the garlic starts to brown. Add the black beans along with a splash of the water from the tin, the dried chillies and the cumin. Continue to cook for a few minutes, then add the chopped tomatoes. Season once more and simmer for 15 minutes until slightly reduced, then serve with a dollop of crème fraîche.

SAUSAGE CASSOULET

Using chipolatas instead of sausages and a beef stock cube to mimic the taste of a slowly simmered casserole drastically cuts down the time it takes to prepare this warm and comforting Sausage Cassoulet. To add texture, I like to finish the dish with a crunchy crouton topping.

To make 1 portion

3 chipolatas

½ red onion, sliced

200g butter beans (from a 400g tin), drained

200g chopped tomatoes (from a 400g tin)

½ beef stock cube

Handful of stale bread, torn into chunks

Pinch of dried oregano

Olive oil

Salt and pepper

To cook

Preheat your oven to 190°C/gas mark 5.

Grab an ovenproof pan and start by pan-frying the chipolatas over a medium heat for about 10 minutes. Once they have started to brown, add the sliced onion and a splash of oil and pan-fry for a few more minutes until softened. Add the beans and chopped tomatoes, season with salt and pepper, crumble in the stock cube and stir. Top with the bread chunks, seasoning them with salt, pepper and oregano and a generous glug of olive oil.

Bake the cassoulet in the oven for 20 minutes until the bread topping turns a lovely golden brown.

ASIAN STUFFED PEPPERS

Sesame oil, garlic and chilli are the key flavours that make the most regular of ingredients into tasty Far-Eastern dishes. Here, I have added those flavours to regular minced beef to create these amazing stuffed peppers.

To make 1 portion

¼ red onion, sliced

Sesame oil

75g minced beef

1 garlic clove, sliced

A few dried chillies (or dried chilli flakes)

1 red pepper

½ spring onion, thinly sliced lengthways

Pinch of sesame seeds

Salt and pepper

To cook

Preheat your oven to 190°C/gas mark 5.

Pan-fry the onion in a splash of sesame oil over a medium heat for a couple of minutes until softened, then throw in the minced beef, season with salt and pepper and continue to fry for about 5 minutes, breaking up the mince with a wooden spoon, until it starts to brown.

Add the garlic, dried chillies and a splash more sesame oil then fry for a minute or two until the garlic starts to brown. At this point, cut the pepper in half lengthways, remove the seeds and stuff it with the minced beef filling.

Place the stuffed pepper halves back into the pan (if the pan is ovenproof) or pop them in an ovenproof dish and bake in the oven for about 15 minutes. Once the pepper is cooked, garnish with spring onion and sesame seeds, then serve.

FILO NACHOS

I wanted to create a really simple nacho dish that could be cooked from scratch using just one pan. The sauce was the easy bit – I've made it hundreds of times before – but to create that distinctive nacho crunch, I had to improvise and luckily hit upon a quirky shortcut of using filo pastry.

To make 1 portion

¼ red onion, sliced

100g minced beef

1 tsp ground cumin

Pinch of dried chilli flakes

¼ red pepper, diced

200g chopped tomatoes (from a 400g tin)

2 sheets of filo pastry, cut into triangles

Small handful of grated Cheddar cheese

1 tsp crème fraîche

½ spring onion, sliced

Olive oil

Salt and pepper

To cook

Preheat your oven to 190°C/gas mark 5.

Fry the onion in an ovenproof pan* in a splash of olive oil over a medium heat. Once the onion has softened, season with salt and pepper, add the minced beef and fry for about 6 minutes until it starts to brown. Stir in the cumin, chilli flakes and diced pepper. Fry for a few more minutes then add the chopped tomatoes and simmer for 5 minutes until the sauce has thickened slightly. Remove from the heat and top with the filo pastry triangles then drizzle with olive oil and scatter over the grated cheese. Bake in the oven for about 10 minutes or until the filo is crispy and the cheese has melted.

Serve topped with the crème fraîche and spring onion.

* If you don't have a pan with an ovenproof handle, then just use your normal pan and transfer the minced beef filling to an ovenproof dish before adding the filo triangles and grated cheese.

ROAST GAZPACHO SOUP

My £1 version of a classic Spanish gazpacho is served hot instead of cold, using oven-roasted peppers, tomatoes, onions and garlic to create a thick and hearty soup. Roasting the ingredients in olive oil, salt and pepper gives the soup a much deeper, concentrated flavour.

To make 1 portion

1 red pepper, roughly chopped

1 big tomato, roughly chopped

1 red onion, roughly chopped

2 garlic cloves, whole

2 slices of bread

Olive oil

Salt and pepper

To cook

Preheat your oven to 190°C/gas mark 5.

Oven-roast the pepper, tomato, onion and garlic in a big glug of olive oil with a generous seasoning of salt and pepper for 20 minutes. Halfway through cooking, sprinkle the bread with olive oil and salt, then place on a wire rack in the oven to lightly toast.

When the vegetables are soft and cooked, add them to a blender (including any roasting juices), squeezing out the soft roasted garlic from each clove and discarding the skins. Blitz to create a soup, adding a splash of water and a big glug of olive oil until it reaches your desired consistency.

Serve the soup with the toasted bread and a sprinkle of pepper.

SPAGHETTI WITH LEMON & PEA PESTO

This refreshing summer pasta dish uses vibrant green frozen peas, tangy parmesan and a squeeze of lemon juice to create a quick and easy pesto sauce.

To make 1 portion

125g spaghetti

Handful of frozen peas

½ lemon

Small handful of grated parmesan

Olive oil

Salt and pepper

To cook

Cook the spaghetti in a pan of salted boiling water.

While the spaghetti's cooking, defrost and warm up the peas in a colander under a hot tap. Set a few peas aside and blitz the rest in a blender with a squeeze of lemon juice, most of the parmesan, a generous glug of olive oil and a pinch of salt and pepper.

When the pasta is cooked, remove it from the water using tongs and mix it in a bowl with the pea pesto sauce and the reserved peas. Add a tablespoon of the pasta cooking water to loosen the sauce and serve sprinkled with the rest of the parmesan.

VEGETABLE CURRY

Everybody should have a speedy vegetable curry recipe in their repertoire. It's a great way to use up leftover veg and make sure you get your five-a-day. This recipe is versatile and can be made with many different vegetables, but I always like to add chunky potatoes so that I don't need to boil any rice – this just makes life so much easier.

To make 1 portion

1 onion, sliced

1 potato, cut into big chunks

1 garlic clove, sliced

A few dried chillies (or dried chilli flakes)

200g chopped tomatoes (from a 400g tin)

2 tsp curry powder

Handful of frozen peas

Olive oil

Salt and pepper

To cook

Pan-fry the onion, potato chunks and garlic in a splash of olive oil over a medium heat, seasoned generously with salt and pepper, for a few minutes until the garlic starts to colour and the onions have softened. Add the dried chillies, chopped tomatoes, a splash of water and the curry powder and simmer for about 10 minutes until the potatoes are cooked and the sauce has reduced. Taste, season again if required, throw in the peas and simmer for a minute or two until cooked, then serve.

GLAZED CHICKEN & SWEET PEA STIR-FRY

One of my favourite things about Chinese cooking are those sweet, sticky glazes, so I've created a stir-fry that is all sticky glaze, made with some really simple crunchy veg and crispy-skinned chicken.

To make 1 portion

1 chicken thigh, de-boned

Sesame oil

1 garlic clove, sliced

A few dried chillies (or dried chilli flakes)

2 tbsp soy sauce

2 tbsp honey

Handful of mangetout

Salt and pepper

To cook

Season the chicken thigh with salt and pepper. Pan-fry it, skin-side down, in a splash of sesame oil over a medium heat. After about 7 minutes, when the skin is golden brown, turn it over and cook it for a further 7 minutes until it is cooked through.

Throw the garlic into the pan and fry for a minute or two until it starts to brown, then add 2 tablespoons of sesame oil, the dried chillies, soy sauce and honey, along with the mangetout. Simmer for a few minutes to thicken the sauce until it has a syrupy consistency, then serve.

AUBERGINE SCHNITZEL

One of the tricks to creating a £1 meal is to take a familiar dish like pork schnitzel and substitute the main ingredient. Here, I've used aubergine instead of pork, then added more flavour to the breadcrumbs to make this dish even tastier than the original.

To make 1 portion

1 tbsp plain flour

1cm-thick slice of aubergine, cut lengthways

1 egg

Handful of breadcrumbs (grated stale bread)

1 tsp dried oregano

1 tbsp grated parmesan

1 tomato, roughly chopped

Small handful of spinach

Wedge of lemon

Olive oil

Salt and pepper

To cook

Season the flour with salt and pepper then dust the aubergine in the seasoned flour. Crack the egg into a bowl and put the breadcrumbs in another bowl with the oregano and parmesan. Dip the floured aubergine into the egg, then into the seasoned breadcrumbs to coat.

Pan-fry the aubergine gently in a generous glug of olive oil over a low-medium heat for 10 minutes on each side until golden brown on both sides and cooked through. Remove the aubergine from the pan, wipe the pan clean, then throw in the roughly chopped tomato and spinach with a splash of oil and fry for 1 minute. Squeeze the lemon over the tomato and spinach mixture, remove from the pan just as the spinach starts to wilt, season with salt and pepper and serve with the aubergine.

ONE-PAN LASAGNE

I love lasagne, but there are so many time-consuming steps that it isn't really a viable weeknight option any more. So, I decided to create a One-Pan Lasagne that cut out all the hassle. It might only have one layer, but the top layer of a lasagne is the best layer, and this is ALL top layer.

To make 1 portion

½ onion, sliced

125g minced beef

1 garlic clove, sliced

200g chopped tomatoes (from a 400g tin)

Pinch of dried oregano

3 dried lasagne sheets

3 tbsp crème fraîche

Handful of grated Cheddar cheese

Olive oil

Salt and pepper

To cook

Preheat your oven to 190°C/gas mark 5.

Fry the onion in an ovenproof pan* in a splash of olive oil over a medium heat for a few minutes until softened. Add the minced beef, season with salt and pepper and fry for about 10 minutes until the meat starts to brown. Add the garlic and fry until it also starts to brown, then add the chopped tomatoes and simmer for about 10 minutes to reduce the sauce a little. Season to taste with salt and pepper and add the oregano. Lay the lasagne sheets on top in a single layer, snapping off the corners and edges so they fit snugly in the pan. Spread the crème fraîche on top and sprinkle over the cheese. Cook in the oven for about 20 minutes until the cheese is nicely melted, then serve.

* If you don't have a pan with an ovenproof handle, then just use your normal pan and transfer the minced beef and tomato mixture to an ovenproof dish before adding the lasagne sheets, crème fraîche and cheese.

STICKY AUBERGINE

This intricately presented Japanese-style aubergine is actually really easy to prepare. Just score the aubergine flesh and mix up a simple glaze to create this stunning vegetarian dish.

To make 1 portion

1 aubergine, halved lengthways

1 tbsp sesame oil

1 tbsp honey

1 tbsp soy sauce

Pinch of dried chilli flakes

1 garlic clove, crushed

Pinch of sesame seeds

½ spring onion, thinly sliced lengthways

To cook

Preheat your oven to 190°C/gas mark 5.

Score the aubergine flesh of both halves in a diamond pattern, making sure you don't cut through the skin, and put them on a roasting tray cut-side up.

Mix together the sesame oil, honey, soy sauce, chilli flakes and garlic in a bowl to create the glaze. Spoon the glaze over the aubergine halves and sprinkle with the sesame seeds, saving a little bit of the glaze for later.

Roast the aubergine in the oven for about 30 minutes, until it takes on a lovely golden brown colour.

Serve the aubergine with a garnish of spring onion and a drizzle of the remaining glaze.

GOATS' CHEESE AL FORNO

I always keep a stash of breadcrumbs in the kitchen so I can throw together simple dishes like this and top them with a crunchy garlic and herb topping. I just love the contrasting textures and the way they can elevate a few simple ingredients into an exciting main meal.

To make 1 portion

200g chopped tomatoes (from a 400g tin)

2 pinches of dried oregano

A few slices of goats' cheese

Handful of breadcrumbs (grated stale bread)

1 garlic clove, crushed

Olive oil

Salt and pepper

To cook

Preheat your oven to 190°C/gas mark 5.

Tip the chopped tomatoes into an ovenproof dish, mix in a pinch of the oregano and season with salt and pepper. Place the goats' cheese slices around the dish.

Mix together the breadcrumbs with a glug of olive oil, the crushed garlic and remaining oregano and season with salt and pepper. Sprinkle the breadcrumb mixture on top of each slice of goats' cheese and bake in the oven for 20 minutes until the breadcrumb topping is golden brown.

CHILLI LAMB NOODLES

This dish has all my favourite Far Eastern flavours: I love the classic garlic and sesame oil combination along with the heat from the dried chillies. For me, these three ingredients are the key to making quick and tasty street-food-style dishes in your own home.

To make 1 portion

¼ red onion, sliced

Sesame oil

75g minced lamb

1 garlic clove, sliced

Handful of dried chillies

Soy sauce

Sheet of extra-thin dried rice noodles

¼ spring onion, sliced into matchsticks

Salt and pepper

To cook

Pan-fry the red onion in a splash of sesame oil over a medium heat for a few minutes until softened. Add the minced lamb, season with salt and pepper and continue to fry for a few minutes, breaking up the mince with a wooden spoon, until it starts to brown. Next, add the garlic and chillies and continue frying until the garlic starts to brown, then add the soy sauce and a splash more sesame oil.

Meanwhile, submerge the noodles in a heatproof bowl of just-boiled water for a few minutes until cooked, then drain and dress them in a splash of sesame oil.

Serve the lamb on a bed of noodles garnished with the spring onion.

BBQ LENTILS & BACON

This super-fast recipe manages to create that authentic sticky, sweet and smoky barbecue effect just by using the oven and two surprise ingredients – sugar and tomato ketchup.

To make 1 portion

200g cooked green lentils (from a 400g tin), drained

1 tbsp tomato ketchup

½ tsp ground cumin

½ tsp smoked paprika

Pinch of dried chilli flakes

1 tsp brown sugar

2 rashers of smoked streaky bacon

Olive oil

Salt and pepper

To cook

Preheat your oven to 190°C/gas mark 5.

Grab an ovenproof dish and mix together the lentils, ketchup, cumin, paprika, chilli flakes and brown sugar. Season with salt and pepper then top with the bacon. Drizzle the bacon lightly with a little olive oil.

Cook in the oven for about 15 minutes, until the bacon is cooked and the lentils have started to caramelise.

Remove from the oven and tuck in.

CHICKEN ISKENDER

Ages ago I went to a posh kebab shop and ate this amazing tomatoey chicken dish that had chopped up pitta bread in it. I'd never seen anything like it before and I never forgot it! So I decided to recreate it using beautiful crisp garlic-infused chunks of bread fried in the meat juices, then smothered in a rich tomato sauce and topped with a dollop of yogurt.

To make 1 portion

1 chicken thigh, de-boned

Handful of crusty stale bread, cubed

1 garlic clove, sliced

Pinch of dried oregano

150g passata (from a 400g tin)

Pinch of dried chilli flakes

2 tbsp yogurt (or crème fraîche)

Olive oil

Salt and pepper

To cook

Season the chicken thigh with salt and pepper. Pan-fry it, skin-side down, in a splash of olive oil over a medium heat. After about 7 minutes, when the skin is golden brown, turn it over and cook it for a further 7 minutes. Add a splash more olive oil and throw in the cubed bread, season well with salt and pepper and add the garlic and the oregano, tossing the bread to evenly coat it in the oil. Fry the bread for a few minutes, and once it is golden brown and the chicken is cooked through, transfer the chicken and bread to a plate, leaving the garlic and the pan juices behind.

Add the passata and chilli flakes to the pan, season again, and simmer for a minute or two to infuse the passata with the chicken and garlic flavours in the pan. When the sauce has thickened slightly, pour it over the chicken and bread, then spoon over the yogurt. Sprinkle with cracked black pepper, drizzle with olive oil and serve straightaway.

SAUTEED MUSHROOM COUSCOUS

Pan-fried mushrooms have a gorgeous nutty flavour and dark colour that, when paired with red onion and spinach, creates a more wintry vibe. Here I have added couscous to make a lovely one-pan meal with very minimal effort but maximum impact on the plate.

To make 1 portion

Handful of mushrooms, sliced

½ red onion, sliced

Handful of spinach

1 egg-cup of couscous

1 egg-cup of water

Olive oil

Salt and pepper

To cook

Pan-fry the mushrooms and red onion together in a splash of olive oil over a medium heat. After about 10 minutes, once the mushrooms are dark in colour, add the spinach, a splash more oil, season with salt and pepper and wilt in the pan for a minute. Remove from the heat, and while the pan is still hot, throw in the couscous, then add the water, give it a quick stir and set the pan aside for a few minutes. Once the couscous plumps up it's ready to serve.

SUN-DRIED TOMATO & FETA YORKIE

Here's a great recipe for using up leftovers: you don't have to use feta and sun-dried tomatoes, just throw in whatever you have. Here, I've cooked the Yorkie using the leftover oil from the tomato jar.

To make 1 portion

A few sun-dried tomatoes (plus the oil)

40g plain flour

60ml milk

1 egg

Chunks of feta cheese

½ spring onion, sliced

Salt and pepper

To cook

Preheat your oven to 190°C/gas mark 5.

Pour enough of the oil from the sun-dried tomato jar into a small ovenproof dish to reach a depth of 1cm and heat it in the oven for about 10 minutes. Meanwhile, whisk the flour, milk and egg in a bowl or jug to make the batter and add a pinch of salt.

When the oil is smoking hot, remove the dish from the oven and carefully pour in the batter. Throw the feta chunks into the middle of the dish, along with a few sun-dried tomatoes and the sliced spring onion. Place back in the oven and cook for about 30 minutes until golden brown (do not open the oven door during the first 20 minutes or your Yorkshire may collapse!). Sprinkle with pepper and serve straightaway.

KEEMA LAMB TACOS

Making your own tortillas is a great way to eat on a budget. They are really simple to make, cost pennies and make a little filling go a long way. Here, I have put my favourite keema lamb curry in a taco, Mexican street-food style.

To make 1 portion

40g plain flour, plus extra for dusting

25ml cold water

½ red onion, sliced

75g minced lamb

1 tsp curry powder

Small handful of spinach

1 tbsp yogurt (or crème fraîche)

1 spring onion, sliced lengthways

Olive oil

Salt and pepper

To cook

Mix the flour and water in a bowl with a pinch of salt to form a dough. Knead on a floured work surface for a minute or two until you get a smooth dough. Cut it into three balls and roll each ball out into a roughly 10cm circle.

Heat a dry frying pan over a high heat, add a circle of dough and cook for 2 minutes on each side, until nicely toasted. Set to one side and repeat with the remaining dough.

Pan-fry the onion in a splash of olive oil over a medium heat for a few minutes until softened, then add the lamb, season with salt and pepper, add the curry powder and cook for about 10 minutes. When the lamb is cooked, throw in the spinach and let it wilt.

Now, assemble the tacos. Spoon some filling onto each taco, drizzle with yogurt and top with spring onion.

FRENCH ONION SOUP

Try serving this soup in a hollowed-out bread roll. It works perfectly because the lid can be turned into a giant cheesy crouton. This is a simplified version of a classic recipe, but you could add a splash of cognac if you want it to taste like it does in France.

To make 1 portion

2 onions, sliced

1 tsp butter

1 tsp sugar

1 garlic clove, sliced

Pinch of dried oregano

1 tsp plain flour

1 beef (or vegetable) stock cube

400ml water

1 bread roll

Small handful of grated Cheddar cheese

Olive oil

Salt and pepper

To cook

Pan-fry the onions with a splash of olive oil, the butter and the sugar over a low-medium heat for 15–20 minutes. When the onions are starting to caramelise, season with salt and pepper, add the garlic, and once the garlic starts to brown, throw in the oregano and flour. Stir for a minute then crumble in the stock cube and pour in the water. Simmer over a medium heat until reduced by about a quarter. Preheat the grill.

While the soup is reducing, slice the top off the bread roll and hollow it out. Sprinkle grated cheese over the cut side of the bread lid and heat under the grill until the cheese is melted. Fill the roll with the soup, season if required and serve with the cheesy toasted bread lid.

SOUTHERN-FRIED CAULIFLOWER

Cauliflower is such a versatile ingredient – it can be used in loads of different recipes in really varied ways. That's the key to One Pound Meals: always ask yourself 'what can I make tomorrow with my leftover ingredients?'. Here, I've given a thick slice of cauliflower a Southern-fried coating and put it on top of a delicious, warm sweetcorn relish.

To make 1 portion

2 tbsp plain flour

1 tsp cajun spice mix

1 egg, beaten

1 thick slice of cauliflower

½ spring onion, sliced

A few dried chillies (or dried chilli flakes)

2 tbsp tinned sweetcorn

2 tbsp honey

Olive oil

Salt and pepper

To cook

Preheat your oven to 190°C/gas mark 5 (if you want to oven-bake the cauliflower instead of frying it).

Season the flour with salt, pepper and the cajun spice mix and put it in a wide, shallow bowl, and put the beaten egg in another wide bowl. Coat the slice of cauliflower with the seasoned flour, pat to remove any excess flour, then dip it into beaten egg (making sure to cover all sides). Put it back into the bowl of cajun-spiced flour and coat all over.

Pan-fry the coated cauliflower in a splash of olive oil over a medium heat for about 7 minutes on each side, or oven-bake it for about 20 minutes on a baking tray, until golden brown and cooked through.

To make the salsa, pan-fry the spring onion in a splash of olive oil along with the dried chillies over a medium heat for a minute or two, then add the sweetcorn, along with 2 tablespoons of liquid from the tin, and the honey. Simmer until the sauce is thick and sticky, season with salt and pepper then serve with the cauliflower.

CHEESY HAM & LEEK PIE

This is comfort food at its best! A luxuriously gooey cheesy sauce with a flaky pastry lid and all made with the very minimum of effort. Using regular sandwich ham, this recipe shows that cooking on a budget does not have to compromise on your enjoyment of food.

To make 1 portion

½ leek, chopped

1 tsp plain flour

200ml milk, plus extra for brushing

Handful of grated mature Cheddar cheese

1 slice of thick-cut ham, torn into chunks

1 small square of puff pastry

Olive oil

Salt and pepper

To cook

Preheat your oven to 190°C/gas mark 5.

Fry the chopped leek in an ovenproof dish or pan* in a splash of olive oil over a medium heat for a few minutes until soft. Add the flour and cook for a further minute. Gradually add the milk, stirring continuously, and cook until you have a smooth sauce. Remove from the heat, stir in the cheese, season with salt and pepper and add the ham.

Top the filling with a piece of puff pastry cut to the same size as the top of the dish or pan, brush it with milk, score it lightly in a criss-cross pattern to make it look pretty, and bake for about 20 minutes, until golden brown on top.

* If you don't have a pan with an ovenproof handle, then just use your normal pan and transfer the filling to an ovenproof dish before adding the puff pastry lid.

PADRON 'POPPERS' & TOMATO

In America there's a popular dish called 'poppers' where small peppers are stuffed with cream cheese, coated in breadcrumbs and fried. This is my far healthier, quicker and easier £1 version, using feta and padron peppers.

To make 1 portion

3 padron peppers, halved lengthways

Small handful of crumbled feta cheese

Small handful of breadcrumbs (grated stale bread)

2 tomatoes, diced

½ red onion, diced

Olive oil

Salt and pepper

To cook

Preheat your oven to 190°C/gas mark 5.

Push the halved padron peppers onto two skewers simultaneously, with the skewers parallel but a distance apart, so that the peppers will stay flat. Stuff each half with feta. Season the breadcrumbs with salt and pepper and sprinkle them on top of the cheese. Drizzle with olive oil and cook in the oven on a baking tray for 15 minutes, or until the breadcrumbs start to brown.

Meanwhile, mix the diced tomatoes with the diced onion, drizzle with olive oil and season with salt and pepper. Place the skewered, stuffed peppers on top of the salad and serve.

SMOKED MACKEREL & KALE CARBONARA

Smoked mackerel is such a meaty fish that you can totally use it as a substitute for bacon in my £1 carbonara. It also doesn't need cooking, so this recipe is way easier than the traditional bacon version.

To make 1 portion

125g dried spaghetti

Handful of kale

2 egg yolks

Small handful of grated parmesan

50g smoked mackerel, flaked

Olive oil

Salt and pepper

To cook

Bring a large pan of salted water to the boil and cook the spaghetti until al dente, throwing in the kale about 2 minutes before it's ready.

Meanwhile, grab a bowl and mix the egg yolks with the grated parmesan and plenty of cracked black pepper. When the spaghetti and kale are cooked, transfer them to the bowl using tongs and mix everything together (the heat of the spaghetti will cook the egg yolk and create the sauce). Add a tablespoon of the cooking water to the pasta along with the flaked smoked mackerel, season if required, and serve with a drizzle of olive oil.

RADIATOR FOCACCIA

You're not going to believe that you can make such beautiful bread so easily. I've even taken out all the kneading steps so you won't get your worktop messy. This really is the simplest bread you'll ever attempt and your radiator does most of the hard work for you.

To make 1 portion

250g strong flour

200ml lukewarm water

7g sachet of dried yeast

A few cherry tomatoes (on the vine)

A few spring onions

1 tsp dried oregano

Olive oil

Salt and pepper

To cook

Grab a bowl and throw in the flour, water and yeast along with a big pinch of salt. Mix it all together using a spoon to create a wet dough. Transfer the dough to an oiled baking tray, wrap with cling film and place in a warm place, like next to a radiator, for 1 hour.

Preheat your oven to 190°C/gas mark 5.

After the dough has risen, unwrap the tray, drizzle over some olive oil and spread the dough out to fill the whole tray. Make lots of indentations in the dough using your fingertips then add the tomatoes and spring onions, pushing them into the dough. Sprinkle over some salt and pepper, along with the oregano and a splash more olive oil, then bake in the oven for 25 minutes until golden brown.

#vegetarian #casual

CRISPY KALE OVEN OMELETTE

One day I was experimenting with making different flavours of kale crisps and stumbled on an idea for a kale-crisp oven omelette. It's a really simple recipe where all the different textures and flavours come together in the oven to produce an amazing dish.

To make 1 portion

2 eggs

Handful of kale

Small handful of grated parmesan

Olive oil

Black pepper

To cook

Preheat your oven to 190°C/gas mark 5.

Whisk the eggs in a small ovenproof dish. Throw the kale on top and sprinkle with the grated parmesan and some pepper, then drizzle with olive oil. Cook in the oven for about 15 minutes until the kale is crispy and the eggs are cooked.

CHORIZO DUMPLINGS

Instead of just being an accompaniment, the dumplings in this recipe are actually the main event. They are made with chorizo and are great dipped into the rich bean and tomato sauce.

To make I portion

½ onion, sliced

1 garlic clove, sliced

200g cannellini beans (from a 400g tin), drained

200g chopped tomatoes (from a 400g tin)

120g self-raising flour

2 tsp butter

20g chorizo, finely diced

A little grated Cheddar cheese

Olive oil

Salt and pepper

To cook

Preheat your oven to 190°C/gas mark 5.

Grab an ovenproof pan* and fry the onion and garlic in a splash of olive oil over a medium heat for a few minutes. Just as the garlic starts to brown, add the beans, chopped tomatoes and a tiny splash of water. Season with salt and pepper and simmer gently over a low heat for about 5 minutes while you prepare the dumplings.

Put the self-raising flour in a bowl with the butter and a pinch of salt. Gently combine the butter and flour by crumbling the mixture between your fingers until it's the consistency of wet sand. Add the finely diced chorizo and a small splash of water, then mix to create a crumbly dough. Roll into four balls, place on top of the tomato stew and cook in the oven for about 30 minutes until the dumplings are golden brown, sprinkling the dish with a little grated cheese just before serving.

* If you don't have a pan with an ovenproof handle, then just use your normal pan and transfer the tomato stew to an ovenproof dish before adding the dumpling dough.

OVEN DIM SUM

In my first book I created some amazing pan-fried gyoza with a pasta-style dough. But, to be honest, I very rarely have time to make them, so I decided I needed a new super-fast dim sum recipe that required a lot less effort.

To make 1 portion

3 sheets of filo pastry

Sesame oil

Small handful of cooked and peeled prawns

1 garlic clove, crushed

1 spring onion, sliced

Soy sauce

To cook

Preheat your oven to 190°C/gas mark 5.

Fold the filo sheets to make them 4-layers thick and about 10 x 10cm. Brush them with sesame oil and stuff them into three holes of a Yorkshire pudding tray. Add 2 prawns, a tiny bit of crushed garlic and some slices of spring onion to each one.

Bake in the oven for 20 minutes until the filo pastry is golden brown.

Serve with a soy sauce dip.

PRAWN & LENTIL CURRY

Prawn curries are delicious, but they're always the most expensive curries on a restaurant or takeaway menu. So, grab yourself some frozen prawns and treat yourself to this amazing curry for dinner tonight. You'll only need a few prawns and probably won't need rice because the lentils bulk this dish out nicely.

To make 1 portion

½ onion, sliced

1 garlic clove, sliced

200g cooked green lentils (from a 400g tin), drained

1 tsp curry powder

½ beef stock cube

Handful of cooked and peeled prawns

Splash of single cream

Olive oil

Salt and pepper

To cook

Pan-fry the onion and garlic in a splash of olive oil over a medium heat for a few minutes. Once the onions have softened and the garlic starts to brown, add the lentils and curry powder, crumble in the stock cube and add a splash of water. Simmer for a minute or two, season to taste with salt and pepper then throw in the prawns. After a couple of minutes, once the prawns are heated through, stir in the cream and serve.

5-CLOVE CHICKEN

Chicken legs are a great single-portion alternative to a roast chicken. This dish is for anyone who loves crisp skin and succulent roasted meat. To make things even better, the whole dish is infused with garlic and the potatoes are basted in the chicken fat to make them extra crispy.

To make 1 portion

1 chicken leg

1 potato, cubed

5 garlic cloves

Handful of kale

Olive oil

Salt and pepper

To cook

Preheat your oven to 190°C/gas mark 5.

Grab an ovenproof dish and throw in the chicken leg and cubed potato. Season generously with salt and pepper and drizzle with olive oil. Next, slightly crush the garlic cloves to break the skin (but do not peel them) and throw those in too. Roast in the oven for about 30 minutes, turning the potatoes every so often to coat them in the oil.

Just before you are ready to serve, throw in the kale, season again and coat the kale in the garlic-infused oil from the bottom of the dish and roast for a further 10 minutes.

Remove from the oven and serve.

BACON & WHITE BEAN NO-BLEND SOUP

When I'm at home I try to avoid getting the blender out as it just creates more washing up. This no-blend recipe means I can enjoy a warming, hearty bowl of soup without any of the hassle.

To make 1 portion

¼ onion, sliced

1 garlic clove, sliced

3 rashers of smoked streaky bacon, chopped

200g cannellini beans (from a 400g tin)

½ chicken stock cube

Small handful of spinach

Olive oil

Salt and pepper

To cook

Gently fry the onion in a saucepan with a splash of olive oil over a medium heat. Once it has softened, add the garlic and bacon, then continue to fry for a few minutes. Add the cannellini beans just before the garlic and bacon start to colour, along with half of the liquid from the tin and a splash more water. Crumble in the stock cube and simmer for about 5 minutes until the soup is the required thickness. Season to taste with salt and pepper and add the spinach leaves. Once the leaves have wilted, the soup is ready to serve.

BAKED MOZZARELLA & POLENTA

Give polenta another chance! It's not fiddly and messy if you just follow my shortcut and bake it instead of cooking it on the hob. Literally, just throw it in the oven and it sort of stirs itself.

To make 1 portion

1 egg-cup of polenta

4 egg-cups of milk

Pinch of dried oregano

½ mozzarella ball

100g passata (from a 400g tin)

Olive oil

Salt and pepper

To cook

Preheat your oven to 190°C/gas mark 5.

Grab an ovenproof dish and throw in the polenta, milk and oregano. Season with salt and pepper and bake in the oven for 20 minutes, then put the mozzarella in the middle of the dish and pour the passata around it. Season again and add a glug of olive oil then return to the oven for a further 20 minutes until the mozzarella is melted and the polenta is cooked. Remove from the oven and serve.

ARROZ DE CAMPO

Finishing this dish in the oven not only makes your life easier, it helps the rice take on a gorgeous sticky texture, the chicken skin becomes extra crispy and the onions rise to the top and caramelise beautifully.

To make 1 portion

1 chicken thigh, bone in

½ onion, sliced

¼ red pepper, sliced

¼ mug of arborio rice

½ mug of water

Pinch of turmeric

½ chicken stock cube

Olive oil

Salt and pepper

To cook

Preheat your oven to 190°C/gas mark 5.

Season the chicken thigh with salt and pepper. Fry it skin-side down in an ovenproof pan* in a splash of olive oil over a medium heat. After about 5 minutes, when the skin starts to turn golden brown, turn it over, add the onion and red pepper then continue to fry for a couple more minutes. Next, throw in the rice, water and turmeric, crumble in the stock cube, mix everything together and throw it in the oven for 30 minutes or until the chicken is cooked.

Remove from the oven and dig in.

* If you don't have a pan with an ovenproof handle, then just use your normal pan and transfer everything to an ovenproof dish before baking.

BUTTERNUT BHAJIS

This recipe is my quirky take on the classic onion bhaji. Onion bhajis are very difficult to get right because of the water content in the onions and the need for a deep-fat fryer. So I switched it up to butternut squash, which works brilliantly. Now you can make restaurant-quality bhajis whenever you want using just a few simple ingredients and a frying pan.

To make 1 portion

¼ butternut squash, peeled and grated

2 tbsp plain flour

1 egg

2 tsp curry powder

2 tbsp yogurt

Pinch of dried mint

Olive oil

Salt and pepper

To cook

Mix the grated butternut squash in a bowl with the flour, egg and curry powder, then season with a pinch each of salt and pepper.

Heat a generous glug of olive oil in a frying pan over a medium heat. When it's hot use a spoon to dollop small amounts of the grated butternut squash mixture into the pan and shallow-fry the bhajis for about 4 minutes on each side. Drain on kitchen paper.

Combine the yogurt and dried mint in a bowl to make a cooling dip.

Serve the hot bhajis with the cooling dip.

LEEK TATIN QUICHE

This recipe is essentially a hassle-free crustless quiche shortcut. I love the way you can get a nice bit of colour onto the leek and create an almost tart-tatin effect.

To make I portion

1 leek, cut into 2cm-thick lengths

3 eggs

Olive oil

Salt and pepper

To cook

Grab a really small pan and place the leeks in it, standing them up like soldiers. Drizzle with a generous glug of olive oil, season with salt and pepper and start pan-frying over a medium heat. After about 10 minutes, turn each piece of leek over to cook on the other side.

While the leeks continue cooking, whisk the eggs and season with salt and pepper. Preheat the grill.

Pour the eggs over the leeks. Turn the heat down to low and cook slowly for about 10 minutes until the egg is almost cooked. Place the pan under the hot grill until the top is completely cooked and golden brown. Eat from the pan.

SUPER-EASY EGG NOODLES

You wouldn't think it by seeing how short this recipe is, but I actually spent ages creating the perfect noodle recipe for this book. I wanted to find the quickest and easiest way to create the most authentically flavoured noodles, but using only one pan. So here it is – my Super-Easy Egg Noodles!

To make 1 portion

1 egg

1 sheet of dried egg noodles

Small handful of spinach

1 tsp sesame oil

1 tsp soy sauce

¼ vegetable (or beef) stock cube

Pinch of sesame seeds

To cook

Bring a saucepan of water to the boil and cook the egg for 7 minutes, adding the noodles to the egg pan after 4 minutes so they cook for 3 minutes with the egg, then add the spinach for the last few seconds.

Remove the egg and cool it down by placing it under cold running water.

Using tongs, transfer the noodles and spinach from the pan of water to a bowl and dress with the sesame oil, soy sauce and crumble in the stock cube. Add 1 tablespoon of the cooking water and stir everything together to evenly coat the noodles.

Peel the egg, cut it in half and place it on top of the noodles, sprinkling over the sesame seeds to garnish.

MEGA SPRING ROLL

Oven-baking spring rolls makes them so much healthier. You can make them as big as you want – like this mega meal-in-one – you're only limited by the size of the filo pastry.

To make I portion

2 sheets of filo pastry

Sesame oil

2 spring onions, sliced

½ carrot, cut into matchsticks

Handful of beansprouts

Handful of cooked and peeled prawns

1 garlic clove, crushed

Pinch of Chinese 5-spice

Pinch of sesame seeds

Soy sauce

To cook

Preheat your oven to 190°C/gas mark 5 and line a baking tray with greaseproof paper.

Brush the sheets of filo on both sides with sesame oil and lay them on top of each other on the lined baking tray.

In a bowl, make the filling by mixing together the spring onions, carrot, beansprouts, prawns, crushed garlic and Chinese 5-spice. Add a tiny drizzle of sesame oil and soy sauce, then place the filling in the middle of the filo sheets and enclose it in pastry by bringing three of the corners into the middle, over the filling, and rolling the filled pastry parcel towards the fourth corner. Bake in the oven for about 30 minutes, or until the pastry is golden brown, sprinkle over the sesame seeds, and serve.

SLOPPY GIUSEPPE

Sometimes you just crave pizza flavours in a hearty plate of food, and Sloppy Giuseppe is the perfect topping style for this crustless £1 dish.

To make I portion

75g minced beef

¼ red onion, roughly diced

¼ green pepper, roughly diced

200g passata (from a 400g tin)

¼ mozzarella ball, roughly torn into chunks

1 tsp dried oregano

Olive oil

Salt and pepper

To cook

Preheat your oven to 190°C/gas mark 5.

Season the minced beef with salt and pepper and roll it into little balls.

Grab an ovenproof pan* and pan-fry the meatballs in a glug of olive oil over a medium heat for about 5 minutes. When the beef starts to brown, throw in the onion and green pepper, then fry for a further 5 minutes until the onion starts to colour. Remove the pan from the heat, tip in the passata, chunks of mozzarella, season with salt and pepper and sprinkle over the oregano. Cook in the oven for about 15 minutes until the cheese has melted, then serve.

* If you don't have a pan with an ovenproof handle, then just use your normal pan and transfer the meatballs, onion and pepper to an ovenproof dish before adding the passata, mozzarella, salt, pepper and oregano.

CREAMY LEEKS, PASTA STYLE

This really quick cheat creates carb-free 'pasta' using sliced leeks. It's such a simple dish to create and one that can be served with loads of different pasta sauces.

To make 1 portion

½ leek, cut into long, thin ribbons

A few sun-dried tomatoes, plus the oil from the jar

100ml single cream

Salt and pepper

To cook

Pan-fry the leek ribbons in a splash of the sun-dried tomato oil over a medium heat for about 4 minutes until soft. Season with salt and pepper then stir in the cream and sun-dried tomatoes. Remove from the heat, season to taste and serve immediately.

ASPARAGUS & EGG TART

Adding eggs to a puff pastry tart filling gives it a luxurious texture and taste. The trick is to make the pastry edges thick so the filling doesn't spill out over the sides.

To make 1 portion

1 sheet of puff pastry, cut to roughly 10 x 7cm, plus some extra strips

1 egg, beaten

Small handful of grated Cheddar cheese

A few asparagus spears, snapped in half

Salt and pepper

To cook

Preheat your oven to 190°C/gas mark 5 and line a baking tray with greaseproof paper.

Place the puff pastry rectangle on the lined baking tray then, using strips of puff pastry about 1cm wide, lay a border around the edge to make it double thickness.

Mix the egg and grated cheese together in a bowl, season with salt and pepper and pour the mixture into the centre of the tart. Brush a little of the egg filling onto the edges (to give the pastry a nice brown crust) and top the egg mixture with the asparagus spears. Bake in the oven for about 25 minutes until the filling is cooked and the pastry is golden brown, then serve.

FAUX GNOCCHI WITH PEAS & ASPARAGUS

I love gnocchi, but it's just too time-consuming and messy to make on a weeknight. So, after much testing, I have devised my very own 'faux gnocchi' recipe that might even be tastier than the traditional version!

To make 1 portion

4 egg-cups of semolina flour

2 egg-cups of milk

2 egg-cups of grated parmesan

Handful of frozen peas, defrosted

A couple of asparagus spears, ribboned

Olive oil

Salt and pepper

To cook

Combine the semolina flour, milk and parmesan in a bowl to create a dough. Very gently roll it into a sausage shape, taking care not to compact the dough too much, then cut into gnocchi-sized pieces. Squash each piece slightly with the prongs of a fork to create that classic gnocchi shape.

Pan-fry the gnocchi in a splash of olive oil over a medium heat for 3 minutes on each side until lightly browned, throwing in the defrosted peas and asparagus ribbons (use a potato peeler to create this effect) about halfway through, then season with salt and pepper and serve.

STUFFED CONCHIGLIONI BAKE

This is basically a classic cannelloni recipe that I have adapted to create the ultimate pasta bake. It has all the same flavours but it's way easier, less fiddly and much quicker.

To make I portion

100g ricotta

Handful of spinach

Handful of large conchiglioni

200g passata (from a 400g tin)

1 tsp dried oregano

Olive oil

Salt and pepper

To cook

Preheat your oven to 190°C/gas mark 5.

Mix together the ricotta and spinach in a bowl along with a pinch of salt and pepper (the spinach will wilt when you mix it).

Stuff the conchiglioni pasta shells with the spinach and ricotta filling then place them in an ovenproof dish along with the passata, oregano, a splash of water, a glug of olive oil and a big pinch of salt and pepper. Place any leftover ricotta in the middle and bake in the oven for about 30 minutes until the pasta is cooked, adding a splash more water over the pasta halfway through.

ROAST PORK BELLY

Pork belly is one of my favourite cuts of meat to roast. If you crave crunchy crackling but you're on a budget, then this is definitely the meat for you. Either roast a big slab of pork belly and cut it into portions, or if you're cooking for one, just cut what you need, roast an individual portion and keep the rest in the fridge or freezer.

To make 1 portion

125g pork belly

200g cannellini beans (from a 400g tin), drained

1 spring onion, roughly chopped

1 tsp chicken gravy granules

Olive oil

Salt and pepper

To cook

Preheat your oven to 150°C/gas mark 3.

Rub oil all over the pork belly and season with salt and pepper, then wrap the bottom of the meat in foil, leaving the skin exposed. Place the pork belly in an ovenproof dish skin-side up and roast for 3 hours, until the skin turns crunchy. For the final 15 minutes, unwrap the pork belly and add the beans, spring onion, gravy granules and a splash of water to the dish.

Serve the pork belly on a bed of the beans and spring onion and sprinkle with black pepper.

POKE BOWL

Poke bowls are gaining popularity at the moment and might just become the next big food fad, but they are so expensive to buy ready made I thought I'd have a go and see what I could do for £1. Firstly, I substituted tuna for beetroot, but the biggest breakthrough was using a load of shelled frozen broad beans instead of mega-expensive edamame beans – you honestly can't tell the difference.

To make I portion

½ mug of basmati rice

1 mug of water

1 tbsp balsamic glaze

1 tbsp sesame oil

1 tbsp soy sauce

Small handful of cooked and peeled prawns

½ carrot, ribboned with a potato peeler

1 cooked beetroot, cut into 1cm cubes

Small handful of broad beans, defrosted and shelled

Pinch of sesame seeds

To cook

Put the rice and water in a saucepan and cook over a medium heat with the lid on for about 7 minutes. When all the water has been absorbed and the rice is cooked, remove the lid and allow it to cool before spooning it into a bowl.

Mix the balsamic glaze, sesame oil and soy sauce together to create the dressing.

Place the prawns, carrot ribbons, beetroot cubes and shelled broad beans neatly into the bowl. Sprinkle with sesame seeds and drizzle over the balsamic, sesame oil and soy dressing.

WHITE BEAN DAUPHINOISE

These oven-baked cannellini beans almost turn into mini gnocchi. This dish is packed with flavour and, best of all, it just involves throwing a few ingredients into a dish and letting the oven do all the work for you.

To make 1 portion

200g cannellini beans (from a 400g tin), drained

1 garlic clove, crushed

100ml single cream

Handful of grated parmesan

Salt and pepper

To cook

Preheat your oven to 190°C/gas mark 5.

Throw the cannellini beans into an ovenproof dish with the garlic. Pour over the cream and sprinkle over most of the grated parmesan. Season with salt and pepper then stir everything together and bake in the oven for about 25 minutes. Once cooked, serve sprinkled with the remaining parmesan and some cracked black pepper.

CURRIED FISH & LEEK NOODLES

Frozen fish fillets are an essential ingredient if you want to eat seafood on a budget. Once they're cooked you'd never notice the difference between frozen and fresh and they are a fraction of the price! Here, I have dusted them in curry powder and had a bit of fun creating leek noodles to go with them.

To make 1 portion

1 frozen white fish fillet

1 tsp curry powder

½ leek, sliced lengthways into thick ribbons

Olive oil

Salt and pepper

To cook

Defrost the frozen fish fillet in the fridge overnight.

The next day, season the fish with salt and pepper and dust with the curry powder. Pan-fry it in a splash of olive oil over a medium heat until cooked. It will take about 5 minutes on each side, depending on the thickness of the fillet. Add the leek ribbons to the frying pan to cook them along with the fish.

Serve the fish on a bed of leek noodles.

WHITE FISH CHOWDER

I always have a stash of frozen fish fillets in the freezer for making quick dishes like this. You don't even need to defrost them if you're in a rush: just throw them into this chowder and it all sorts itself out in the end.

To make 1 portion

2 spring onions, sliced

1 tsp butter

1 tsp plain flour

300ml milk

A few potato chunks

1 frozen white fish fillet

1 tsp tinned sweetcorn

Olive oil

Salt and pepper

To cook

Pan-fry the spring onions (keep some back for garnishing) in the butter for about 1 minute over a medium heat, then add the flour and stir it together. Stir in the milk, add the potatoes and simmer for about 10 minutes until the potatoes are almost cooked. At this point, add the fish (add it earlier if it is still frozen) and simmer for a few minutes until the fish is cooked. Throw the sweetcorn in just before serving, season to taste with salt and pepper, then flake the fish and garnish the chowder with the remaining spring onion and drizzle with olive oil.

CHICKEN & CREAMED SPINACH

Creamed spinach is one of my favourite side dishes. Adding crispy-skinned, pan-fried chicken and cannellini beans transforms it into a nicely balanced and delicious main meal.

To make 1 portion

1 chicken thigh, bone in

1 garlic clove, sliced

200g cannellini beans (from a 400g tin), drained

Handful of spinach

75ml single cream

Olive oil

Salt and pepper

To cook

Season the chicken thigh with salt and pepper. Pan-fry it skin-side down in a splash of olive oil over a medium heat. After about 10 minutes, when the skin is golden brown, turn it over and cook it for a further 10 minutes. Add the garlic and, just as it starts to brown, throw in the cannellini beans and then the spinach. Once the spinach has wilted and the chicken is cooked through, pour over the cream, season again with salt and pepper, then simmer for a few minutes to thicken the sauce a bit and serve.

PUFF PASTRY FIORENTINA

I think I might be a bit obsessed with pizza shortcuts and this one is probably my most daring yet. It might look like a regular pizza, but look a little closer and you'll see this one is actually made with puff pastry. Yes, puff pastry!

To make 1 portion

20 x 20cm square of puff pastry

2 tbsp passata

Pinch of dried oregano

¼ mozzarella ball, torn into chunks

A few spinach leaves

1 egg

Salt and pepper

To cook

Preheat your oven to 190°C/gas mark 5 and line a baking tray with greaseproof paper.

Using a plate as a template, cut out a big circular piece from the puff pastry square. Place it on the lined baking tray and lightly score a 1cm border around the edge with a knife, making sure not to cut all the way through. Prick the inner circle a few times with a fork (this will stop it rising in the oven).

Spread the passata onto the pastry, within the border, season with salt and pepper, sprinkle with the oregano then add the mozzarella and spinach. Bake in the oven for about 10 minutes, then crack the egg in the middle and return to the oven for another 10 minutes until the egg white is cooked but the yolk is still runny.

BLACK RICE

This is my £1 recreation of a Spanish dish I had in Seville. I loved it so much that I had to attempt it when I got back to England. I took a few shortcuts and substituted a few ingredients, and as soon as I tried it with black beans as the base, everything just fell into place.

To make 1 portion

1 garlic clove, sliced

200g black beans (from a 400g tin)

¼ mug of long-grain rice

½ mug of water

½ fish stock cube

Handful of cooked and peeled prawns

1 tbsp crème fraîche

Pinch of smoked paprika

Olive oil

Salt and pepper

To cook

Pan-fry the garlic in a splash of olive oil over a medium heat for 1 minute. Just before the garlic starts to brown, add the black beans along with half of the liquid from the tin. Season with salt and pepper and simmer for a few minutes to soften the beans, then mash the mixture with a fork to create a black paste. Add the rice and water, crumble in the stock cube and simmer for about 15 minutes until the rice is cooked, adding a little more water if required.

Throw in the prawns a few minutes before serving, then serve topped with the crème fraîche and sprinkled with the smoked paprika.

PARMESAN-WRAPPED ASPARAGUS

The contrasting flavours and textures in the dish work so well, so when it's asparagus season and you see them at rock-bottom prices, grab a bunch and make loads of these; they're really easy.

To make 1 portion

4 sheets of filo pastry, cut to 10 x 10cm

8 thin asparagus spears (or 4 fat ones)

Small handful of breadcrumbs (grated stale bread)

1 tbsp grated parmesan

Olive oil

Salt and pepper

To cook

Preheat your oven to 190°C/gas mark 5 and line a baking tray with greaseproof paper.

Brush the filo squares with olive oil and fold them in half to create triangles. Loosely wrap the asparagus with the filo and lay them on the lined baking tray. Brush the asparagus with olive oil too (so the breadcrumbs and parmesan stick to the spears) and sprinkle over breadcrumbs, parmesan, and some salt and pepper. Bake in the oven for 15 minutes until the pastry is golden brown, then serve with an extra drizzle of olive oil.

PEA NOODLE SOUP

This summery, vibrant green noodle soup is cooked in one saucepan in just 10 minutes. I love using super-thin rice noodles because they are so quick to cook and create a more delicate dish that works well with the sweet peas.

To make 1 portion

1 garlic clove, sliced

A few dried chillies (or dried chilli flakes)

Sesame oil

300ml water

1 vegetable stock cube

Handful of frozen peas

1 sheet of thin rice noodles

½ spring onion, sliced into long strips

Salt and pepper

To cook

Grab your smallest saucepan and start by frying the garlic and dried chillies gently in a splash of sesame oil over a medium heat. Just before the garlic starts to brown, add the water and crumble in the stock cube, then bring to the boil. Simmer for a few minutes, throw the peas into the pan and bring the water back to the boil, adding the noodles for the last minute or so depending on the instructions on the packet.

Ladle the soup into a bowl, season with salt and pepper and garnish with the sliced spring onion.

SPROUT CAESAR SALAD

This is my take on one of the most famous salads in the world. Using Brussels sprouts and crème fraîche, with plenty of cracked black pepper, I've managed to create a speedy and refreshingly zingy version of the classic caesar.

To make 1 portion

1 rasher of smoked streaky bacon, cut into large pieces

A few chunks of stale bread

Small handful of Brussels sprouts, very thinly sliced

1 tbsp crème fraîche

Olive oil

Salt and pepper

To cook

Pan-fry the bacon in a splash of olive oil over a medium heat. Once the bacon starts to brown, toss in the bread and fry it in the smoky bacon-infused oil until it starts to colour.

Meanwhile, mix the sprouts with the crème fraîche and season them with loads of cracked black pepper (and a tiny pinch of salt if needed).

Serve the bacon and croutons on a bed of the crunchy sprouts to create the perfect summer salad.

CHICKEN & POTATO IN A CREAMY SAUCE

The challenge with cooking a meal in one pan is how to cook the meat, carbs, veg and sauce together but still give each ingredient its own identity. Here, it's all about crisping up those potatoes in the chicken fat, then adding bursts of flavour with sun-dried tomatoes and bringing it all together with a creamy sauce at the last minute.

To make 1 portion

1 chicken thigh, de-boned

1 potato, cubed

1 garlic clove, sliced

A few sun-dried tomatoes

1 spring onion, sliced

75ml single cream

Olive oil

Salt and pepper

To cook

Season the chicken thigh with salt and pepper and pan-fry it, skin-side down, along with the cubed potato, in a generous glug of olive oil over a medium heat. Turn the potatoes every so often, and after about 7 minutes, when the chicken skin is golden brown, flip the chicken over and continue to fry for a further 7 minutes. Add the garlic, sun-dried tomatoes and spring onion, and after a few minutes, once the chicken is cooked through and just as the garlic is starting to brown, pour in the cream. Simmer for a minute or two to thicken the sauce slightly, taste and season once more if required, then serve with a drizzle of olive oil and plenty of cracked black pepper.

CUBETTI HOTPOT

I always want more potatoes with my hotpot, so this is my solution: cut them into cubes and pile them high. This also makes the recipe way less fiddly. To get this dish under £1 I swapped stewing beef for minced beef, which also means the whole thing is ready in a fraction of the time it takes to cook a regular hotpot.

To make 1 portion

½ onion, sliced

125g minced beef

1 garlic clove, sliced

200g chopped tomatoes (from a 400g tin)

½ beef stock cube

1 potato, cubed

Pinch of dried oregano

Olive oil

Salt and pepper

To cook

Preheat your oven to 190°C/gas mark 5.

Fry the onion in an ovenproof frying pan* in a splash of olive oil over a medium heat for a few minutes until softened. Add the minced beef, season with salt and pepper and fry for about 10 minutes until cooked through and nicely browned, adding the garlic about halfway through. Tip in the chopped tomatoes and crumble in the stock cube, then stir and simmer for about 5 minutes until the sauce has reduced. Toss the potato cubes with a drizzle of olive oil, top the minced beef with the potato cubes, season with salt and pepper and sprinkle with the oregano. Bake in the oven for about 35 minutes until the potatoes are golden brown and cooked through.

Serve with plenty of cracked black pepper over the top.

* If you don't have a pan with an ovenproof handle, then just use your normal pan and transfer the minced beef mixture to an ovenproof dish before adding the potato cubes and oregano.

BLACK BEANS & STUFFED PADRON PEPPERS

This is my ultimate Mexican brunch, prepared in the style of a Middle Eastern shakshuka. All the essential Mexican flavours are there, with the cumin and black beans, but what makes this dish such a crowd-pleaser is the unusual feta-stuffed padron peppers.

To make 1 portion

½ red onion, sliced

1 garlic clove, sliced

A few dried chillies (or dried chilli flakes)

200g black beans (from a 400g tin), drained

1 tsp ground cumin

A few padron peppers, halved lengthways

Small handful of feta cheese

Olive oil

Salt and pepper

To cook

Preheat your grill to a medium-high heat.

Pan-fry the onion in a splash of olive oil over a medium heat for a couple of minutes until soft. Add the garlic and fry until it starts to brown, then add the dried chillies, black beans and cumin. Season with salt and pepper and fry for a couple more minutes, then remove from the heat.

Add the padron peppers to the pan, cut-side up, and crumble feta into each one, then drizzle with olive oil. Cook under the grill for a minute or two until the cheese starts to colour and serve straightaway.

#vegetarian #casual

WELSH RAREBIT

Cheese on toast will never be the same again after you've made this. This is next-level cheese on toast and is well worth the extra 30 seconds of effort.

To make 1 portion

Handful of grated mature Cheddar cheese

1 egg-cup of single cream

2 slices of bread

2 spring onions, halved

A few splashes of Worcestershire sauce

Black pepper

To cook

Preheat your grill to high.

Mix the grated cheese and cream together in a bowl to create a cheesy spread with the consistency of mashed potato. Spread it onto the bread slices, top each slice with two halves of spring onion, splash with Worcestershire sauce, then cook under the grill for a few minutes until the cheese melts and starts to brown.

Remove from the grill, sprinkle with cracked black pepper and serve straightaway.

BAKED FETA

Certain cheeses can be baked with spectacular results. It sounds weird, but give this Baked Feta a try: its texture changes and it becomes a luxurious centrepiece to this very simple, rustic dish.

To make 1 portion

100g feta cheese

A few cherry tomatoes (on the vine)

Pinch of dried oregano

Olive oil

Salt and pepper

To cook

Preheat your oven to 190°C/gas mark 5.

Grab an ovenproof dish and throw in the feta and tomatoes, drizzle everything with olive oil and sprinkle with the oregano. Season the tomatoes with salt and pepper, then bake for 25 minutes until the tomatoes are soft and gooey, and the feta is nicely coloured.

CHINESE BOK CHOI

Why not make life a little easier in the kitchen and start incorporating simple one-pan recipes like this into your weekday routine: bok choi isn't just a side dish – throw in some lamb and you've got something quite special.

To make 1 portion

¼ red onion, sliced

Sesame oil

100g minced lamb

1 garlic clove, sliced

Pinch of dried chilli flakes

Soy sauce

½ bok choi, sliced

Salt and pepper

To cook

Pan-fry the onion in a splash of sesame oil over a medium heat until softened, then add the lamb, season with salt and pepper and continue to pan-fry for about 5 minutes until it starts to brown. Add the garlic and chilli flakes and cook for a few minutes until the garlic starts to brown, then add a splash more sesame oil, a splash of soy sauce, a splash of water and the bok choi. When the bok choi has wilted it's time to serve.

SAMOSA TART

I love vegetable samosas, but they are not quite suitable as a standalone main course, so I started experimenting with ways to prepare and present exactly the same ingredients to make it a more substantial dish, and this is what I came up with.

To make 1 portion

2 sheets of filo pastry

¼ red onion, sliced

½ carrot, sliced

A few broccoli florets

Handful of frozen peas

2 tsp curry powder

Olive oil

Salt and pepper

To cook

Preheat your oven to 190°C/gas mark 5.

Brush the sheets of filo pastry with olive oil on both sides and use them to line a small ovenproof dish to create a pie base, scrunching up the edges. Throw in the veg (make sure you cut them thin enough to cook all the way through) then drizzle with olive oil, sprinkle in the curry powder and season with salt and pepper. Bake in the oven for about 20 minutes, until the filo is golden brown and the vegetables are cooked.

PRAWN THERMIDOR

This is my affordable take on the ultra-luxurious and mega-expensive lobster thermidor. If we're being 100% honest, there isn't much difference between whole prawns and chopped-up lobster, so I went full steam ahead and created my own version of lobster thermidor for just £1.

To make 1 portion

½ onion, chopped

1 garlic clove, chopped

Handful of cooked and peeled prawns

200ml single cream

1 tsp paprika

Handful of breadcrumbs (grated stale bread)

Olive oil

Salt and pepper

To cook

Preheat your oven to 190°C/gas mark 5.

Grab an ovenproof frying pan*, add the onion and fry in a splash of olive oil over a medium heat for a couple of minutes. Season with salt and pepper, and once they have softened, add the garlic and continue to fry until the garlic starts to brown. Add the prawns, cream and paprika then simmer for a few minutes until the sauce thickens. Season again if required.

Drizzle the breadcrumbs lightly with olive oil and season with salt and pepper. Top the prawns with the seasoned breadcrumbs and bake in the oven for about 20 minutes, until the breadcrumbs are golden brown, then serve.

* If you don't have a pan with an ovenproof handle, then just use your normal pan and transfer the filling to an ovenproof dish before adding the breadcrumb top.

ROAST SQUASH CARPACCIO

I'm always trying to come up with interesting salad ideas, and this sliced and roasted Squash Carpaccio is a real winner. Slicing the squash thinly means it takes on more flavour and cooks in a fraction of the time it takes to cook heftier chunks, but you don't need fancy knife skills to get this posh-looking effect: just your potato peeler.

To make 1 portion

Handful of thinly cut squash

Splash of balsamic vinegar

Small handful of feta cheese, crumbled

Small handful of rocket leaves

Olive oil

Salt and pepper

To cook

Preheat your oven to 190°C/gas mark 5.

Spread the thinly cut squash over a baking tray. Season with salt and pepper then drizzle over a splash of olive oil and balsamic vinegar. Mix everything together to coat the squash, making sure you spread it out again, and bake for about 15 minutes until the squash is cooked. Transfer the squash to a plate and serve warm with the crumbled feta, another drizzle of olive oil, cracked black pepper and the rocket.

CUMIN-CRUSTED CAULIFLOWER

Cauliflower is really great value for money and a perfect ingredient for One Pound Meals. It is also healthy, versatile and pretty simple to cook, so why not try this quirky cumin-crusted baked cauliflower?

To make 1 portion

1 thick slice of cauliflower

1 tbsp butter

Small handful of breadcrumbs (grated stale bread)

1 tsp ground cumin

Pinch of dried parsley

Olive oil

Salt and pepper

To cook

Preheat your oven to 190°C/gas mark 5.

Butter the slice of cauliflower as you would a slice of toast and place it on a baking tray.

Season the breadcrumbs with salt and pepper and mix them with the cumin, parsley and a glug of olive oil. Sprinkle the breadcrumb mixture over the cauliflower and roast in the oven for about 20 minutes, or until the cauliflower is cooked through and the breadcrumbs are golden brown.

Remove from the oven and serve.

COURGETTE CANNELLONI

This is a lovely veggie dish that looks way more complicated to prepare than it actually is. Using courgette instead of pasta looks impressive and makes the dish taste so much more fresh and vibrant.

To make 1 portion

3 tbsp ricotta

Small handful of spinach

3 wide, long slices of courgette (use a vegetable peeler)

200g passata (from a 400g tin)

1 tsp dried oregano

Small handful of grated Cheddar cheese

Olive oil

Salt and pepper

To cook

Preheat your oven to 190°C/gas mark 5.

Combine the ricotta and spinach in a bowl along with some salt and pepper (the spinach will wilt as you mix it all together).

Divide the ricotta and spinach mixture between each courgette slice and roll them up to create your cannelloni.

Grab a small ovenproof dish and pour in the passata, season with salt and pepper, mix in the oregano, then place the courgette cannelloni on top. Top each cannelloni with grated cheese, drizzle some olive oil over the whole dish, then bake in the oven for about 25 minutes until the courgette is tender.

Remove from the oven and serve.

CHICKEN PARMIGIANA

This is lazy cooking at its tastiest! Crispy potatoes, luxurious melted mozzarella and a tangy tomato sauce all cooked on one tray in the oven.

To make 1 portion

1 chicken thigh, de-boned, skin on

1 potato, cubed

4 tbsp passata

¼ mozzarella ball

1 tsp dried oregano

Olive oil

Salt and pepper

To cook

Preheat your oven to 190°C/gas mark 5.

Place the chicken thigh (skin-side up) and potato cubes on a baking tray, season generously with salt and pepper and drizzle with olive oil. Cook in the oven for about 30 minutes, turning the potato cubes every so often.

When the chicken is cooked and the potatoes are golden brown, spoon the passata over the chicken, top with the mozzarella and sprinkle over the oregano. Return to the oven for a couple of minutes until the mozzarella has melted, then serve.

GNUDI

This is my straightforward take on Italian ricotta dumplings, a delicacy called Gnudi. These delicious parcels have a gnocchi-like texture and are light and fluffy but packed with so much flavour.

To make 1 portion

2 garlic cloves, finely chopped

Handful of spinach, roughly chopped

100g ricotta

2 tbsp semolina flour, plus extra for dusting

2 tbsp grated parmesan

Olive oil

Salt and pepper

To cook

Pan-fry the garlic in a splash of olive oil over a medium heat. Just before the garlic starts to brown, throw in the spinach and continue to fry for a minute more until wilted. Remove from the heat and transfer to a bowl. Once it has cooled a little, add the ricotta, the semolina flour and half the grated parmesan, then season with salt and pepper. Mix to create a light and fluffy dough, then sprinkle some semolina flour onto a plate and dollop separate tablespoons of the mixture onto the plate. Roll them in the flour to create little gnudi.

Pan-fry the gnudi in a splash of olive oil over a medium heat for a few minutes on both sides until they start to brown, then serve with a drizzle of olive oil and a generous sprinkling of the remaining parmesan.

SAVOURY LAMB BAKLAVA

There's always an interesting and fun way to make a pie but call it something far posher. So here is my Savoury Lamb Baklava! It's basically a hybrid of Middle Eastern dishes that creates a moreish pastry-topped delight.

To make 1 portion

½ red onion, sliced

100g minced lamb

1 garlic clove

1 tsp ground cumin

Small handful of spinach

A few sheets of filo pastry

Pinch of sesame seeds

Olive oil

Salt and pepper

To cook

Preheat your oven to 190°C/gas mark 5.

Pan-fry the onion in a splash of olive oil over a medium heat for a couple of minutes. Once the onion has softened, add the lamb and season with salt and pepper. When the lamb starts to brown, throw in the garlic and cumin and continue to fry for about 5 minutes until the lamb is golden brown. Add the spinach and cook for another 30 seconds until wilted.

Fold and cut the filo sheets into rectangles then layer the filo and lamb on a baking tray to create a lasagne effect. Brush with olive oil, sprinkle the top with sesame seeds and bake for 15 minutes until golden brown.

DETROIT PIZZA

This must be the easiest pizza recipe ever. I've taken out every superflous step to create this amazingly simple but really tasty pizza with a characteristic Detroit-style square shape and thick crust.

To make 1 portion

150g self-raising flour, plus extra for dusting

100ml cold water

4 tbsp passata

Pinch of dried oregano

Big handful of grated Cheddar cheese

6 pepperoni slices

Salt and pepper

To cook

Preheat your oven to 190°C/gas mark 5.

Using a spoon, mix the flour and water together in a bowl along with a big pinch of salt to form a dough. Dust the worktop with a little flour then knead the dough on the worktop for a minute or two until smooth. Roll it into a rectangle. Lay the dough onto a 15 x 23cm baking tray (increase the ingredient quantities if you are using a bigger tray) and push the dough into the edges and corners. Spread the passata over the top, leaving a border around the edge, and season with salt and pepper. Sprinkle over the oregano and cheese and top with the pepperoni slices, then bake in the oven for about 20 minutes until the base is cooked and the cheese is nicely melted.

CHEESE & POTATO HOTPOT

I'm using Cheddar here but you can totally throw in any other interesting cheeses that you've got lurking in the fridge. This dish is a great template for using up other leftovers too – imagine adding some layers of Sunday's roast chicken or a few slices of ham like I have here.

To make 1 portion

2 potatoes, very thinly sliced

1 onion, very thinly sliced

A couple of slices of cooked ham, torn into chunks

Big handful of Cheddar cheese, grated

1 tsp dried oregano

Olive oil

Salt and pepper

To cook

Preheat your oven to 190°C/gas mark 5.

Grab an ovenproof dish and start by adding a layer of potato slices, then onion slices and ham, then cheese, with a little salt and pepper and a pinch of oregano. Repeat 4 or 5 times until the dish is full to the top and finish with a layer of potatoes. Drizzle over a little olive oil and bake in the oven for about 30 minutes or until the top layer is golden brown and all the potatoes are cooked.

MEXICAN FRIED BEANS

Something amazing happens when you pan-fry tinned kidney beans: they sort of puff up and split, creating a totally different texture that takes on loads more flavour.

To make 1 portion

200g red kidney beans (from a 400g tin), drained

1 garlic clove, sliced

A few dried chillies (or dried chilli flakes)

1 tsp ground cumin

1 spring onion, sliced

1 egg-cup of couscous

1 egg-cup of water

Olive oil

Salt and pepper

To cook

Pan-fry the kidney beans in a splash of olive oil over a medium-high heat for about 1 minute, season with salt and pepper then add the garlic, dried chillies, cumin and spring onion. When the garlic starts to brown and the kidney bean skins have split, tip everything onto a plate and add the couscous and water to the pan. Turn off the heat and allow the couscous to absorb the water for a few minutes then serve it with the beans.

RAGU DI PORCO

A slow-cooked meat ragu with pappardelle and plenty of parmesan is one of my all-time favourite meals. Using a whole piece of meat instead of mince results in a much more luxurious dish than a standard spag bol.

To make 1 portion

½ onion, sliced

1 garlic clove, sliced

200g chopped tomatoes (from a 400g tin)

1 pork shoulder steak

½ beef stock cube

100ml water

3 dried lasagne sheets

Small handful of grated parmesan

Olive oil

Salt and pepper

To cook

Grab a saucepan or a casserole dish with a lid. Fry the onion in a splash of olive oil over a medium heat until softened, then add the garlic and continue to fry until the garlic starts to brown. Season with salt and pepper, then stir in the chopped tomatoes, add the pork, crumble in the stock cube and pour in the water. Cover and simmer over a low heat for 3 hours, adding a splash more water if required. In the last 5 minutes of cooking, flake the meat apart using a fork and throw the lasagne sheets into the dish to cook with the ragu. Once the lasagne sheets are cooked, serve sprinkled with the parmesan.

PERI PERI TACOS

This is my fresh and vibrant take on peri peri chicken, using crisp lettuce cups and a cooling yogurt dressing to create amazing summer tacos.

To make 1 portion

1 chicken thigh, de-boned

1 tsp hot smoked paprika

1 egg-cup of couscous

2 egg-cups of water

4 lettuce leaves

1 tbsp yogurt

Olive oil

Salt and pepper

To cook

Coat the chicken thigh in a mixture of paprika, a pinch each of salt and pepper and a drizzle of olive oil. Pan-fry the chicken over a low-medium heat, skin-side down first, for 10–12 minutes on each side until cooked through and caramelised on the outside. Remove from the heat and set the chicken to one side.

Add the couscous to the pan (off the heat), along with the water, and stir for a few seconds to incorporate all the pan juices, then leave the couscous to rest for a few minutes and plump up.

Slice the chicken into thin strips, then assemble your tacos by spooning some of the peri peri-infused couscous onto each lettuce leaf, placing some chicken strips on top, then drizzling with the yogurt and sprinkling over some cracked black pepper.

INDEX

First published in 2018 by HEADLINE HOME
An imprint of HEADLINE PUBLISHING GROUP

2

Cataloguing in Publication Data is available from the British Library

ISBN 978 1 4722 5439 9
eISBN 978 1 4722 5438 2

Commissioning Editor: Muna Reyal
Art Direction and Design: Superfantastic
Photography: Dan Jones
Home Economist Assistant: Sophie Garwood
Project Editor: Kate Miles
Copy Editor: Laura Nickoll
Proofreader: Ilona Jasiewicz
Indexer: Caroline Wilding

Bound and printed in Germany by Mohn Media
Colour reproduction by Born London
Typeset in Brandon Grotesque, Avenir, Billabong

HEADLINE PUBLISHING GROUP
An Hachette UK Company
Carmelite House
50 Victoria Embankment
London EC4Y 0DZ

www.headline.co.uk
www.hachette.co.uk